MORE BENCH TIPS
FOR JEWELRY MAKING

Proven Ways to Save Time and Improve Quality

by

Bradford M. Smith

More Bench Tips for Jewelry Making:
Proven Ways to Save Time and Improve Quality

All generally accepted industry safety procedures should be followed when using tools in the jewelry shop. The material in this book should be used only as a learning guide. Nothing in these guidelines is intended to negate the need for proper clothing, masks, goggles, and other protection.

The Author and Publisher disclaim any liability for injuries, unexpected results or problems that might occur while attempting to follow suggestions in this publication.

Copyright © 2018 - Bradford M. Smith

Published by Whimsey Wylde
Santa Monica, CA

ISBN-978-0-9882858-8-0

NOTE: The terms Dremel® and Foredom® used occasionally are registered trademarks of their respective companies.

DEDICATION

This book is dedicated to my loving wife and family. Without their help and support, many of my projects might never blossom. They are a fan club like no other, and I love them dearly. Their fresh ideas and detailed critiques give me the confidence and feedback needed to stay on target with my writing. I am truly blessed.

ALSO BY THE AUTHOR

BENCH TIPS FOR JEWELRY MAKING

ACCESSORIES FOR THE FOREDOM AND DREMEL

MAKING YOUR OWN DESIGN STAMPS

BROOM CASTING FOR CREATIVE JEWELRY

THE RELUCTANT FARMER OF WHIMSEY HILL

http:// amazon.com/author/bradfordsmith

TABLE OF CONTENTS

PREFACE

Accomplished jewelers have a variety of techniques, tools and shortcuts, collectively known as bench tips, that are used to save time and increase the quality of the resulting work. I've always loved these tips and continue to write up the ones I find to be particularly effective. For those who enjoyed my first book, "Bench Tips For Jewelry Making," I'm happy to be able to pass on more of my tips in this volume.

Many of the suggestions presented here are solutions to problems I commonly encounter as a studio jeweler and class and shop instructor. The solutions often draw upon my background in manufacturing technology and small lot production techniques.

The material in these bench tips should be used only as a learning guide. Nothing in these tips is intended to negate the need for proper clothing, dust masks, and eye protection. All generally accepted industry safety procedures should be followed when using tools in the jewelry shop.

Happy hammering!

   - Brad

WARNING

Metal Working Tools and Procedures Are Dangerous

Do not attempt procedures described in this book
without professional supervision.

All local and industry safety procedures
should be followed.

Chapter 1

STONESETTING TIPS

FLUSH SET BURNISHER

Making your own burnisher for flush setting of round faceted stones is quick and easy. Start with an old 1/8 inch steel bur shaft. File a 3/8 inch long taper with a sharp point on the working end. This can be done by hand with a file or by spinning the bur shaft in the flexshaft and holding the file to it.

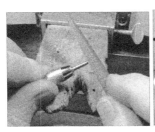 

Next, sand the taper smooth and round off the tip so it will not scratch the stone or jab your finger. Finally, polish the end well with Tripoli or Zam on the buffer.

Finish off the burnisher by clamping the bur shaft in a sturdy handle that will hold it firmly. My preference is a file handle or pin vise that will clamp the 1/8 inch bur shaft securely.

For more on the flush setting process, there are some good tutorials on the Internet that describe the process.

LEARN TO CUT & POLISH

Knowing how to shape and polish your own gemstones opens up many new possibilities for solving problems with setting a stone, but lapidary equipment can be quite expensive and classes hard to find.

Many people are able to solve both problems by joining a local gem and mineral club. These clubs are inexpensive to join, have members who are expert at cutting & polishing, and offer monthly speaker programs on interesting topics. Some clubs arrange workshops where members teach various skills. Others have free lending libraries of books & videos. And some even have their own shop facilities, fully equipped for cutting, polishing and jewelry making.

To find a rock & gem club in your area, see some of the contact addresses in the Appendix or do an Internet search for "gem mineral club" along with your Zip Code.

PREPARING BEZEL ENDS FOR SOLDERING

You should not have to buy an eighty-dollar miter vise in order to sand or file a straight edge on a ring band or a bezel. My students encounter this problem frequently, and here's how to solve it with either a fine-cut file or a sanding board.

Be sure to use a file or sanding board that is considerably wider than the metal being filed. When filing the end of the strip, pay close attention to the angle of the file.

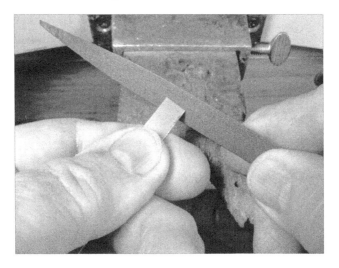

If the file is used back-and-forth like this, any slight change in the angle of your arm will trim off material from the corners of the strip. This will create a gap at both ends of the joint and make it difficult to get a quality solder joint.

By changing the angle of filing to up-and-down, the sanding stick will produce a straight edge on end of the strip without any rounded corners.

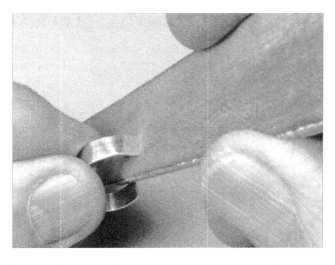

Note that the file or sanding stick used should be wider than the strip. This technique works well on bezel strips and ring bands.

QUICKLY FORM A SMALL BEZEL

Forming a bezel strip around a cabochon gets more difficult for me with small stones, like less than 8mm.

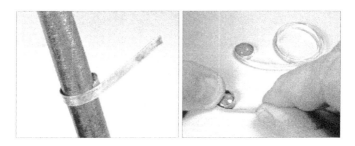

My solution is to pre-form the end of the strip into a circle a little smaller than the stone, push the circle down over the stone, shape the strip to the stone, and mark where to cut.

A small rod or small mandrel will work well for the pre-forming, but a small tapered mandrel, round or oval, is a wonderful addition to any jewelers toolbox.

REMOVING A CABOCHON FROM A BEZEL

In order to open up the bezel to remove a stone, you have to stretch the top edge of it quite a bit - like opening up a draw-string bag. A sharp blade can be used to tease the edge of the bezel out a bit from the stone. Make sure to go around gently several times.

Then use a thicker blade to open the bezel enough to remove the stone. Try to not pry too much in any one place. The bezel can tear easily. And be careful to not scratch the stone.

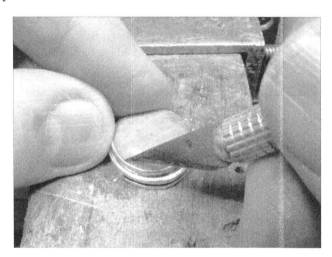

BEZEL TOO SMALL

After a bezel has been soldered to the baseplate and is found to be a little too small or when a stone doesn't quite fit into a cast setting, the easiest fix is often to make the cabochon a little smaller.

Take a careful look at the shape of the bottom edge of the cabochon. Sometimes the lower-most corner can be filed off a bit to make the stone smaller. It is important that all file marks will be covered by the bezel once the cab is seated in the bezel.

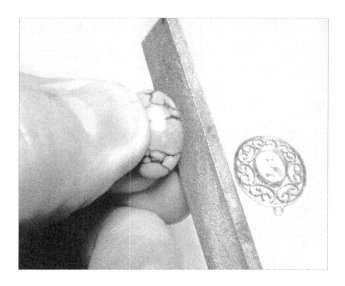

A diamond file with a width of 10-15mm is the best choice for reshaping a stone. If you don't have one, see if the local store carries ruby nail files. Ruby is #8 on the hardness scale and works well on quartz, jasper and softer stones.

Remember to round off the bottom edge of the stone to allow space for any little bits of solder that might be in the setting. These can put undue stresses on the stone as the bezel walls are burnished down.

HOLDING ODD SHAPES

Sometimes two hands are needed to work on a stone setting, as when using a bezel punch or when hammer setting a stone, and often the geometry of a piece rules out using a vise or clamp. In these situations one of the most versatile materials is an inexpensive thermoplastic that can be melted in hot water, by a heat gun, or with a gentle torch.

Jewelry supply companies are a good source for the material, but it can also be purchased in small or large quantities on the Internet. Search on the keyword "thermoplastic."

A convenient way to use the thermoplastic is to use it on your bench pin. Start with a spare bench pin and hollow out a shallow pocket to hold the plastic. Carve the pocket about12mm deep and remove a little extra wood around the sides at the bottom. This will help lock the plastic into the pocket.

Then melt enough of the plastic to fill the pocket. One choice is to use a small Butane torch, but the plastic can also be dropped into a cup of hot water, or the granules can be heated with a heat gun. Harbor Freight has the guns at a very good price.

MAKING MULTIPLE BEZELS

When making several bezels all the same size, it makes sense to use a method so that each will turn out the same and not require any modification. One way to do this is to determine the exact length of the strip to cut.

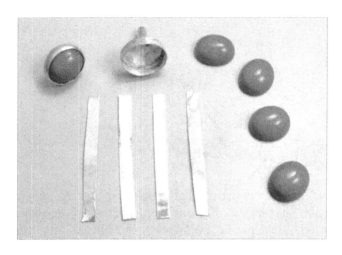

Do this by measuring the first bezel before soldering it. After soldering, do a trial fit with the stone and adjust the measurement if needed for a perfect fit. Then cut lengths of bezel strip for the remaining stones and fabricate all the bezels in one batch.

ODD SHAPED MULTIPLE BEZELS

Often a project will require two or more bezels of an odd shape, not round or oval. My solution is to shape a mandrel just for the job out of a piece of plastic or aluminum. Either material files easily, doesn't rust, and is readily available locally or from online sources like Ebay.

The two shapes on the lower left of this picture were formed on the aluminum mandrel that is shown on the right. They are used in the perfume bottle design as sidewalls for the through holes that pierce the water-tight container.

SETTING A CAB WITH A ROUNDED BOTTOM

Most cabochons are cut with flat bottoms for easy setting, but some will be cut with a belly on the bottom, possibly to increase the weight of stones that are sold by the carat or gram. For whatever reason, rounded bottoms make bezel setting difficult because any effort to close the bezel causes the stone to tilt.

One easy way to bezel set such a stone is to make a jump ring big enough to seat around the inside edge of the bezel. This supports the stone as the bezel is closed around the edge. Choose a wire just thick enough to keep the center of the stone from touching the bottom of the bezel cup.

TRANSPARENT CABS

When bezel setting a transparent cabochon in silver, I usually cut out the back of the bezel to allow background light to show off the colors and patterns in the stone. If this is not possible or appropriate, I worry that the silver bezel will tarnish under the stone and will ruin its brilliance.

One solution is to place a piece of thin silver Mylar plastic under the stone to act as a mirror that will never tarnish. Mylar is readily available in craft and gift wrap stores or in a pinch from a party balloon supplier. You may even want to experiment with using colored or patterned Mylar (i.e. diffraction pattern) under some stones.

Chapter 2

FABRICATION TIPS

CURVED TUBE BAIL

Many jewelry makers like to use a short length of curved tubing as a bail, but it's quite difficult to bend tubing

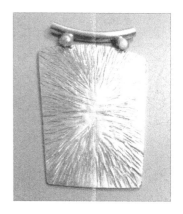

However, short segments of tubing already bent can be purchased in any bead supply catalog or store. Using one of these avoids having to buy a whole length of commercial tubing and attempt to bend it.

ANNEALING THIN WIRE

Annealing thin gauge wire can be tricky. For a good anneal, all areas of the wire must be heated uniformly to just barely red and then as it cools to black, immediately quench it in water.

It's easy to melt a section of the wire if you're heating with a torch. Avoid problems by winding the wire into a tight coil about two inches in diameter. Fasten the coil in two or three places with scrap wire.

Risk of melting the wire can be minimized by using an oven set at about 1150 F. Place the coil of wire into the heated oven, let it soak for 5-8 minutes, and quench.

If no oven is available, place the coil in a small metal can (like tuna fish comes in), cover with a sheet of metal, and heat with the torch from the bottom.

DRILLING A HOLE

Some drilled holes do not require much accuracy, such as for threading a saw blade through to pierce a shape. But others may need to be positioned accurately, or have an exact diameter, or be drilled at a precise angle. In these situations, here are some tricks to use to ensure the hole is formed correctly.

Position – Scribe fine guide lines with a sharp pointed tool for the target, mark the location with a center punch, check the divot is on target, and move the divot if necessary with another strike.

Size – Start with a small drill, one that is considerably smaller than the final size of the hole. Inspect the hole for being exactly on target. Move the hole if necessary with a small cylindrical bur. Finally, enlarge it in steps to the desired final size.

Angle – Most holes can be drilled by eye, but those with special requirements on their angle should be done in a drill press.

And remember when drilling, it's important to use good quality drills. Low cost steels will not hold up. Best results are with drills from jewelry or machinist supply companies, not discount stores. And be sure to use a lubricant (wax or oil) for best results.

FANCY HINGE PINS

Some hinge designs, such as those used for a box or a locket, are primarily functional and are somewhat hidden from view. But others hinge designs, like those used on a bracelet, are in full view and call for a more elegant approach.

One way to achieve this is to add small balls to the hinge pins. The usual technique is to melt the ends of the pins with a small and very hot torch to form the ball. However, it's fairly difficult to achieve nicely rounded shapes and even more difficult to consistently make all balled ends look the same.

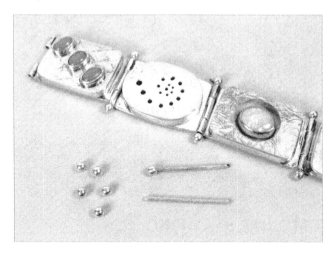

My approach is to purchase round silver beads that are soldered onto the ends of each hinge pin. In this example, the hinge pins are 18ga wire, and the beads are 3mm. The holes in the beads may have to be enlarged to ensure a good fit with the wire. This can be done by hand with a tapered reamer, but a drill will also work.

FILEWORK

Filework is a technique that can be used to create bold, sculptured elements on some jewelry designs.

The repeating patterns are created with just a hand saw and various files, and finishing goes quickly with sanding discs and polishing wheels on the flexshaft.

The pattern is started by scribing equally spaced lines. Then a fine saw blade is used to start each repeating notch which is then refined with needle files. A few example designs are shown above. Others can be found with an Internet search on "filework."

LAST MINUTE STAMPING

Many times I've forgotten to stamp a piece until it's almost done. At that stage, the problem is finding a way to support the piece to avoid deforming it when you hit the stamp.

If the stone has not been set, one of the easiest places to do your stamping is on the back side of the bezel. Invert the bezel onto a steel rod held in the bench vise. The rod will support the bezel as you hammer the stamp on the back.

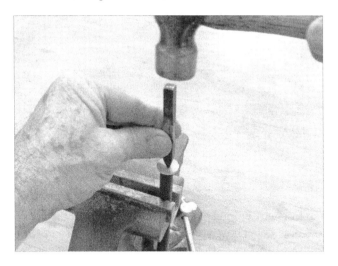

I keep a couple different sized round punches for just this kind of work, but any piece of steel will work so long as it fits inside the bezel. To avoid any scratching or denting of the bezel by the punch, file the face of the punch flat, sand it smooth, and polish with Zam or Tripoli on the buffer.

FITTING A BEZEL TO A CURVED SURFACE

When soldering a large bezel to a bracelet, it is difficult to get the two pieces to fit closely. Any gap between the two (see arrows) will make soldering difficult.

Trying to saw or file the bottom of the bezel quickly distorts its shape. One good way to shape the bottom of the bezel is to use a sanding drum on the Foredom or Dremel. Just sand a bit and do a test fit, sand and fit, etc.

Once the fit is close, look carefully at the points of the bezel which touch the bracelet. These are the areas which have to be removed to close the adjacent gaps. If an even better fit is needed, support the bracelet in a vise or on a mandrel, tape a piece of sandpaper grit side up in the area where the bezel will be attached, and use the bracelet shape to sand the bottom of the bezel for a perfect fit.

MAKING FILIGREE WIRE

Making the twisted wire for filigree is not as difficult as one may think. Use a double strand of 24-26 gauge silver wire, twist it tightly. Then flatten it a bit.

Filigree looks best when the wire has a very tight twist. Start with dead soft wire and twist a double strand until it breaks. (It seems to break on one end or the other, hardly ever in the middle) Then to get a real tight twist, anneal the wire and twist it a second time until it breaks.

A screw gun or a flexshaft saves a lot of work when twisting wire, but do not use an electric drill as it turns too fast and is difficult to control. Keep a little tension on the wires as you twist.

The final step in preparing filigree wire is to flatten it slightly either with a planishing hammer or a rolling mill. The amount of flattening is a personal preference. I flatten the wire about 25%. The wire will be quite stiff at this point, so it's best to anneal it again before starting to form the filigree shapes.

MULTIPLE ANNEALINGS

Certain processes like forging, roll printing, foldforming, and making sheet from an ingot all require frequent annealings. While this can be done with a torch, an oven offers an easier and better solution if you have a lot of annealings to do.

The temperature can be controlled better than with a torch, and the cost is reasonable when compared with the price of torch gasses these days. So when doing a lot of work with copper or silver, turn the oven on to about 1150 F and save a lot of time.

ROLL PRINTED TEXTURES

If you have access to a rolling mill, roll printing is an easy way to add interesting textures to copper, brass or silver sheet. A texture is formed on the sheet metal by pressing a pattern material into it. But a lot of pressure is required, and that is why a rolling mill is the best piece of equipment to use.

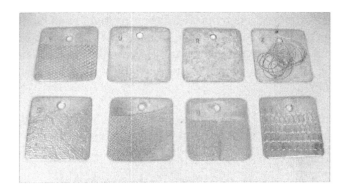

The process is quite easy.

1. Make up your sandwich of annealed sheet and pattern

2. Put it in the mill and close the rollers on it

3. Extract the sandwich by rolling it backwards out of the mill

4. Close the rollers enough to impress the pattern deep enough

5. Roll the sandwich through the mill without stopping

The major challenge is with Step #4, and that's where you will have to do some experimenting. The amount of compression will be different for every new pattern material. Use scrap copper sheet to try out a pattern before committing to silver. Try rolling just a small amount of the sandwich, and then reverse and roll it back out to inspect how well the pattern is being impressed into the metal. Adjust the compression, carefully reassemble the sandwich and roll through.

My favorite pattern materials are those that have actual holes in it, like plastic or aluminum window screening , lace, cup cake wrappers on Amazon, or the plastic mesh used to pack fruit in grocery stores. For a more subtle texture, try coarse rice paper from an art store, the paper with big fibers in it. manila file folder sheet also makes a great pattern. Cut or punch holes in it, and polish your metal sheet before pattern rolling it. Experimentation will turn up all sorts of novel textures to decorate your work.

18

One caution with pattern materials - never let any steel pattern touch your rollers. It could damage them. Steel can be used as pattern material but always shield it from touching the rollers with a sheet of scrap copper or nickel.

SEED CHAIN

For me one of the most difficult steps in weaving a chainmail design is getting it started. Once underway, the design is typically just a repetition of a few steps, but the first inch or so is usually a challenge.

An easy way to avoid having to figure it out each time is to save a short length of the chain to be used as a "seed" to start the next one you construct.

Of my favorite designs, the Vipera Berus is particularly difficult to get started. The last time I did one, I started by making an inch or two of the design using some brass jump rings. Then I switched to using silver rings to finish the project. When done, I disconnected the brass section and saved it as my "seed" for the next time I do that design.

SMALL PARTS CONTAINERS

Jewelers have a continuing need for small containers to organize and store the many little parts and tools we deal with in making jewelry. This is especially true if you travel back and forth to classes and workshops.

One good find are plastic vials about 15 mm in diameter and 75 mm long. The best part is they are available free in large numbers. The vials are used in the healthcare field for drawing blood samples. They cannot be used after their expiration date, and are thrown out. On my last visit to the doctor, I asked the nurse if they had any expired vials. The answer was "How many do you want?", and she tried to give me 400 of them. We settled on just 200 that I shared with my students.

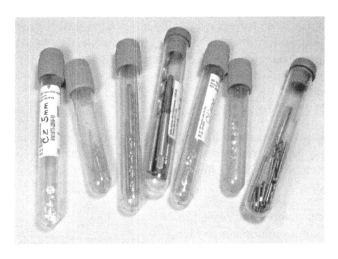

The ones I have are called "Vacutainers" but there are probably many other names. They are clear plastic with a rubber stopper and a paper label all ready to write on. I find them really handy for small parts like jump rings, prong settings, small drills, nuts & bolts, faceted stones, and precious metal filings.

SMOOTHING SMALL PIERCED HOLES

Piercings on a sheet form add elegance and detail to a jewelry item, but the sharp interior edges can be a little difficult to finish. There are two ways that can be used. The first is a strip of 600 grit sandpaper mounted in a saw frame and threaded through the piercing. The sandpaper can be reinforced with a piece of shipping tape (the kind with threads in it) on the back side. Then cut into thin strips about 3/16 to 1/4 inch.

A second way to smooth out irregularities in small pierced holes is to make a needle burnisher for use in a Foredom or Dremel tool. Start with good quality steel such as in an old 3/32 inch bur shaft or twist drill.

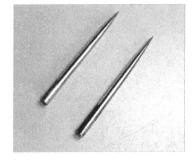

The burnisher can be shaped with a file and sandpaper. After a fine sanding, round off the point a bit to prevent injuries, and give the burnisher a high polish with Tripoli or Zam.

A quicker way to shape the tapered part of the needle is to grip the shaft in a motor tool and hold a file to it while it spins.

When using this tool, be sure to use a little lubricant. Light strokes are all that is needed to burnish down any rough areas.

STIPPLED TEXTURE

Stippling is a texture applied with a pointed punch. It's quick and easy. A centerpunch, hammer and bench block is all that is needed. Hold the piece flat on the bench block when lightly tapping with a hammer to avoid bending the metal.

A faster method to stipple is to use a hammer handpiece fitted with a pointed anvil. The anvil is easily shaped from a spare tip. Mount it in a pin vise and grind the tip to a point. Take care not to overheat the point. Overheating can destroy the hardness of the tip. Keep it cool with an occasional dip in some water. Finish up by sanding the tip and polishing it with Zam or Tripoli.

With the hammer handpiece, applying the texture is as easy as painting it on. Sketch a design and then "paint" between the lines (See the copper box lid in the background above) or even sign your name. Don't forget to back your piece with a bench block.

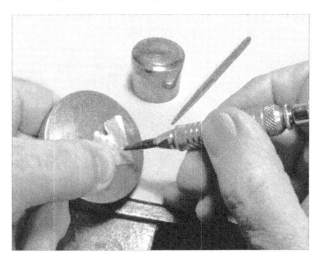

TAPERED REAMERS

A tapered reamer is a very useful tool when working with the small diameter tubing or when sizing the diameter of holes for riveting.

After sawing or filing small diameter tubing, reamers quickly help to clean burrs out of the inside hole. They are also useful when preparing holes for riveting. If the correct drill size is not available, just use a smaller drill and ream the hole to the correct size

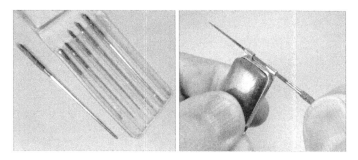

Reamers are a must-have tool when making hinges. They can be used to correct misalignments in two or more knuckles or to enlarge the hole in the knuckles for a perfect fit with the hinge pin.

WOOD-PECKERING

When drilling a deep hole in metals (more than four drill diameters) be sure to use some oil as a lubricant and a wood-peckering motion with the drill. The combination keeps the drill cooler and helps clear the chips from the hole.

Wood-peckering is a term I use for drilling a little, withdrawing from the hole, drilling a little deeper, withdrawing, etc. The periodic withdrawing from the hole helps to clear away the chips and reduce friction which can stress the drill shaft to the breaking point. Wood-peckering also helps keep the drill tip lubricated so it runs cooler and keeps its sharp cutting edges longer.

THREADED FASTENERS

Threaded fasteners (nuts and bolts) are a great way to join components where the heat of soldering cannot be used or when the jewelry item may need to be disassembled for cleaning or maintenance.

Different sizes of fasteners can be found in any hardware store. Brass screws solder easily and will not rust. Head designs are available in a variety of shapes - slotted, Allen-head, Phillips-head, hexagonal, flat, or round.

For instance, the silver conchos on this leather hatband are attached with size 10-32 flat-head brass screws soldered to each concho. That allows them to be quickly removed for polishing.

This ring uses miniature screws that allow it to be disassembled for polishing of the middle brass component. Flat-head screws give a nice look to this ring and will not snag a thread on fabric that might rub against it.

THREADING A HOLE

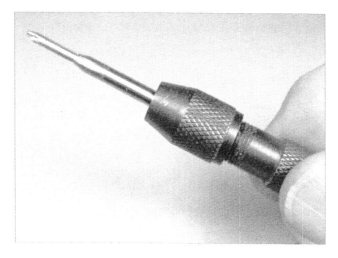

Threads can be cut with a tap into a drilled hole. As you might guess, the hole must be exactly the right size for the threading to work correctly. Once the size of the thread to use has been selected, do an Internet search for "Tap Drill Chart" to determine the correct drill size to use.

The process is straightforward. Locate the position of the hole, centerpunch it, drill a small pilot hole, and enlarge the pilot to the finished tap drill size. Then clamp the tap into a hand vise or tap holder, insert it into the hole, lubricate with some oil, push downward, and screw it in clockwise. Be sure to keep the tap at a perfect right angle to the surface of the metal.

Every turn or two, back the tap out at least a half of a revolution to break the chips, and then resume cutting clockwise until finished. Test with a bolt to check that the thread works properly.

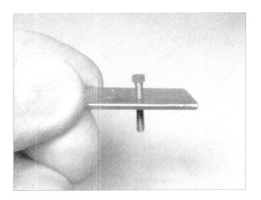

This fileworked ring mentioned earlier is held together with small screws. The holes in the brass component are tapped to act as the "nuts" for holding the piece together. Using the small 00-90 screws makes it easy to disassemble the ring in order to polish the brass center.

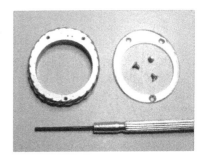

Threaded components are readily available in a variety of sizes. Some can be found in local hardware stores, but the smaller sizes must be ordered from specialty suppliers such as:

- http://scalehardware.com
- http://jimorrisco.com
- http://metalliferous.com
- http://microfasteners.com
- http://rtlfasteners.com

When ordering, consider the diameter of the screw, the length of the threaded body that will be needed, the type of head geometry desired, and any matching components required like nuts, washers, screwdrivers, or taps.

Chapter 3

SOLDERING TIPS

HEATING FROM UNDERNEATH

Beginners concerned with the cost of silver often cut the baseplate for a project very close to the bezel. While this minimizes scrap, it usually makes the job of soldering very difficult because much more torch skill is needed to heat the baseplate up to soldering temperature without melting the bezel. I usually leave 6-7mm of the baseplate showing on all sides of the bezel for an easy soldering from the top.

But for those situations where there is a risk of melting some feature, such as fancy gallery wire, the wise choice is to heat from the bottom. Tripod screens suck a lot of heat out of the flame, so I use small strips of titanium bent into V-shapes to elevate the item and allow the flame to get under the piece. Titanium will not solder and will not melt at the temperatures used in our jewelry work.

FILLING A HOLE

Sometimes while constructing a piece or finishing a casting, a hole or dimple will be discovered that needs to be filled. Everyone who has tried flowing a little solder into one of these defects knows that it rarely works. Silver solder doesn't seem to fill small holes unless you give it some help. Here's how to do it.

For a small hole, I use a drill to enlarge it and make the cavity round. It's best to choose a drill that is a good fit for a standard size wire. If that is not possible, sand a slight taper on the end of a larger wire and push it into the drilled hole. Then add a little solder around the base of the wire and heat.

To fill a dimple, I place solder into the cavity, add a scrap of silver sheet that is big enough to cover the dimple, and solder. After pickling, file and sand off the excess metal and polish smooth.

FINDING FIRESTAIN

Firestain occurs when Sterling silver is heated too hot or too many times. Under these conditions oxides form below the surface of the metal. The gray or purplish stain is most easily seen with light bounced off a piece of white paper.

There is no easy solution for removing firestain short of sanding or aggressive polishing, but it can be prevented.

FIRESTAIN PREVENTION

To prevent firestain when soldering Sterling, consider using the Prips mixture. It is named for Jack Prip, who taught at the University of Rochester, NY. The mixture he developed was 3 parts boric acid, 2 parts borax and 2 parts tri-sodium phosphate. Grind finely and dissolve in warm water. In use, parts are brushed or dipped and dried with a torch. Then they are positioned for soldering, and solder & flux are added.

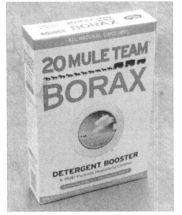

Borax and boric acid can be found at most jewelry supply companies. Often borax can be found in local stores as 40 Mule Team laundry soap. And boric acid can often be found locally as cockroach killer (look carefully at the list of ingredients).

Whenever heating an alloy that has a lot of copper in it (copper, brass, bronze, nickel silver, 14K gold), a black copper oxide forms on the surface and will inhibit the solder from flowing.

Various fluxes or fire coat solutions can be used to protect the surface of the metal to avoid the oxide. Liquid flux will work, paste flux will work, and a number of commercial firecoats are available from supply companies. The Prips mixture easy, low in cost, and very effective.

Goldsmiths like a traditional mixture of boric acid and alcohol. The borax in the Prips mixture gives better protection at the higher temperatures.

MAKE SOLDERING CLAMPS

Some soldering jobs are easy, and others test your creativity. Holding parts in place with clamping tweezers often acts as a heat sink to make matters worse, but small clamps can be formed from titanium strip to help solve the most difficult problems.

Titanium is a handy metal to use at the solder station because it cannot be melted by the torches we use, and no solder will stick to it. Titanium also retains its strength at high temperatures much better than steel. These properties make it an excellent metal for supporting and clamping items at the solder station.

Strips of titanium can be purchased from the Knew Concepts Company or from Ebay. A convenient size is 7mm wide and 18 to 20 gauge thick. It is easily sheared, sawed, ground or filed to the shape needed.

SOLDERING HINGE KNUCKLES

When fabricating a hinge, small segments of tubing are soldered onto each of the two elements to be joined. Each segment of tubing becomes one knuckle of the hinge joint, and each knuckle is positioned so that it fits in between (or meshes with) the knuckles of the other element.

Hinges should be fabricated to function as smoothly as those on the doors of a cabinet or a house. A good hinge should rotate freely and not flex in any other direction. To get this result, there should be a good fit between the knuckles and the pin. The knuckles of the two elements of the hinge should mesh closely together, and the holes in the knuckles should align with each other so a hinge slides in easily.

Choosing the size of the tubing and the wire for a hinge pin solves some of these requirements. Typical wire sizes are 18ga, 16ga or

14ga. Choose one and search for tubing with an inside diameter that is only 0.1mm or .004 inch larger than the wire diameter.

Note that one side of a hinge usually has a single long knuckle that is soldered in the center, and the other side has two shorter knuckles soldered onto the ends of the hinge.

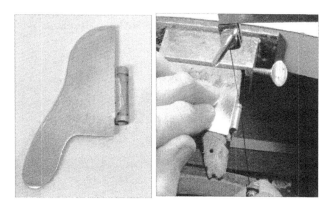

Finishing and fitting the knuckles must be done carefully. I like to start with the center knuckle. Mark its final size and saw off excess tubing leaving just a half millimeter on each end. A fine blade like 6/0 works best on thin tubing walls. Finish the center knuckle by filing the ends square and to the exact length needed.

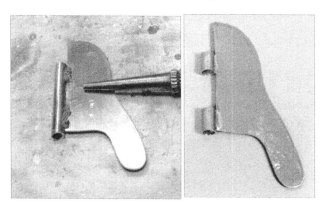

A good way to ensure the two outer knuckles are in alignment is to start by soldering a single piece of tubing the full length between the two outer knuckles.

Align the two halves of the hinge next to each other and mark where the center cavity needs to be cut out. When sawing, be sure to leave the cavity a little short on each end. Then carefully file the cavity to exactly the correct size so it meshes closely with the mating center knuckle of the hinge.

This guarantees that the holes through the two end knuckles will line up and the pin will insert straight through all elements of the hinge.

STURDY SOLDER PICK

Everyone has a favorite solder pick. For many operations, a light, fine-pointed pick makes delicate work a pleasure. But there are times when a stronger pick is needed to apply pressure.

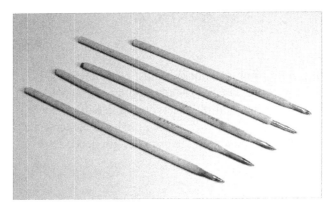

For these occasions, a nice pick can be made from a repurposed welding rod. Simply cut the rod to a convenient length, remove a bit of the flux material from one end, and file the end to a point. The welding flux provides nice insulation from the heat.

Chapter 4

MATERIALS TIPS

METALS ANALYSIS

If knowing the metal content of a piece is important, take the piece into a local coin shop or possibly a store that advertises "We Buy Gold." Most of these stores now have a hand-held tester called an XRF, (X-Ray Fluorescence analyzer). Point it at the metal, and it displays the amount of 8-10 common metallic elements that are typically in jewelry metals. Results are displayed as percentages of gold, silver, platinum, rhodium, copper, nickel, zinc, lead, etc.

MIXING EPOXY

For epoxy to harden as expected, the amounts of the two components must be equal, and this is not always what comes out when you squeeze one of the common twin-tube packages of epoxies I get at the hardware store.

My preference is to split the package down the middle by sawing though the center of the package and the caps with a jewelers saw.

Being able to handle each tube separately lets me more accurately control the amount dispensed.

DISSOLVING EPOXY

An epoxy bond can be broken with heat or with a strong solvent. The material starts to lose its strength around 400 F, but often that is too hot for adjoining components. In those situations, a solvent like Attack or straight acetone from a hardware or paint store can be used.

Using a solvent will not be quick, and it produces fumes you may not want in your home. A safe and easy way to soak a piece for a while is to pour enough solvent to cover the epoxy bond into a large jar and cap it off to contain the evaporation.

WHAT'S IN A NICKEL

Students often ask about using a coin in their jewelry or for something at the soldering station. But in the USA coins can be deceiving - nickels have very little nickel in them and copper pennies have almost no copper in them.

The consequence is that a penny used to hold up an end of a sheet at the solder station will melt and damage your jewelry work before the solder gets hot enough to melt. Why? Because it's zinc.

To find answers about what is in a coin, do an Internet search for "metal content of coins". There are many sites, but one good one is http://en.wikipedia.org/wiki/Coins_of_the_United_States_dollar

Chapter 5

TOOL TIPS

BRACELET MANDREL HOLDER

A bracelet mandrel is usually held in a vise to free up both hands
for holding the workpiece and forming it into final shape. But this
isn't always possible at workshops or demonstrations where only a
conference table is provided. In these situations, a wooden holder
can be constructed to cradle the mandrel and hold it in proper
position for pounding.

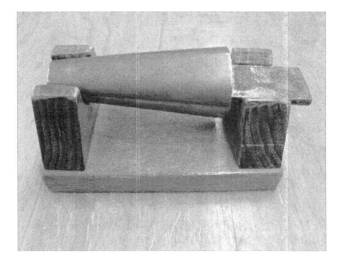

This one was made with the help of a band saw. Materials are
some scraps of 2x4 and a 1x6 board for the base. Each mandrel
will be a little different in size, shape, and holding surface, so the
end pieces of 2x4 will have to be shaped to match. The pictures
that follow show how it can be approached.

You might ask a friend who does woodwork.

Notches are cut into one end to hold the mandrel at various angles. Here are views of the two positions I use the most.

CORE DRILL BLOCKAGE

When using small core drill bits (1mm – 3mm), stone debris will build up inside the bit. This debris has all the small granules of stone that the diamond abrasive has ground out of the hole and may have pieces of the solid inner core that is left by the hole in the core drill. If not cleaned out, the debris will quickly clog the core drill like concrete, and drilling progress will stop.

To deal with this problem, look for core drills that are hollow all the way through. Designs with only one open end can be very difficult to clean out. A hollow tube can usually be cleared with a piece of steel wire or a broken drill shank pushed through from the back. For instance, use an 18ga steel wire to clear a 2.5mm OD core drill. If the hole in the drill is pretty well compacted, a small twist drill might help to free it.

Sometimes a chunk of the solid inner core breaks off inside the drill, and it is pretty hard to get it out. To avoid this, withdraw from the hole and try to break off any piece of the core that can be seen in the hole. A steel dental pick or an awl works well to break the core out of smaller holes. Then fish out the loose piece with tweezers or by tapping the stone upside down.

CUSTOM STAMPS

Using design stamps to add texture or embellish your jewelry is fast and easy. Stamps can be found at many of the popular jewelry supply companies, and there are large and active user group communities on Facebook, Instagram and Pinterest who share ideas, techniques, and examples of finished work.

Facebook groups in this area include:

Let's Make Jewelry
Metal Stamp Addicts
The House of Stamps
Metal Stamps, Tools, and Dies

There are also a number of impressive independent artists offering sets of unique custom stamp designs to choose from:

Bear Skull Stamps - Israel Delgadillo
    BlackBearSkull@aol.com

Buffalo Rutland Company - Cody Rutland
    BuffaloRutlandCompany.com/portfolio.html

David Tarver
    David.Tarver@angelo.edu

Ferro Valley Tool - Danny Wade
    FerroValleyTools.com

Oregon Trail Metal Stamps - Roberta Pihl
    OregonTrailSilver.com

Ortega Sculpture - Hector Ortega
    OrtegaSculpture.com

DRESSING NEW TOOLS

Most new hand tools when purchased should be examined closely for sharp edges and surface defects that might leave marks on your jewelry items. While obvious with a tool like a burnisher, the procedure applies equally to any tool surface that will touch your metal. Pliers and hammers, clamps and calipers all need to have their sharp edges softened. And the tips of many new burnishers are so sharp as to create a nasty gash if the tool slips.

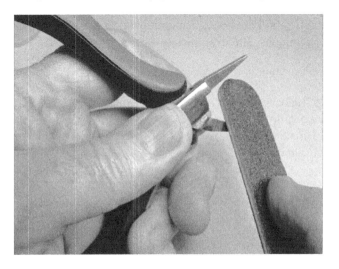

I call the process "dressing". It can usually be done quickly with a medium flat file followed by a sanding stick. However, it is often easier to use an abrasive stick than it would be to use a file.

The objective is not to remove a lot of metal or to change the basic shape of the tool, but rather just to remove burrs, scratches or edges that might slice your finger. For most tools, smoothing to the 600 grit level is sufficient, but a better polish is needed on burnishers and the faces of punches and hammers. This can be done most easily with the Tripoli or Zam wheel on your buffer.

FLAT LAP SANDING

When sanding the backs of pieces, loose sandpaper or sanding sticks are apt to round off edges or leave an uneven surface. The job goes much faster if the sandpaper is attached to a flat surface and the piece is rubbed against it. The technique works really well, gives a good quality surface, and does not risk scratching the top side of the item.

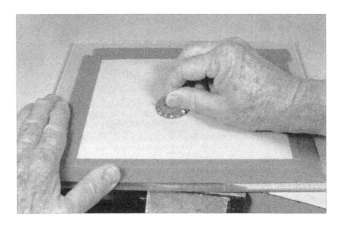

But clearing the work bench and fastening the sandpaper is a pain. A more versatile approach is to tape sheets of your favorite sandpaper onto sheets of plastic. Other good choices for the flat base are 1/8 inch metal, or 1/4 inch glass, or Masonite. This allows easy storage of the sheets when they are not needed.

JUMP RING CUTTER

When making a lot of jump rings, the bulk of the work is cutting them off the coil. Power attachments for the flexshaft are available, but they are an expensive tool for jewelers who use just a moderate number of jump rings.

A grooved wooden block worked well for me to hold the coils while cutting, but it was a little awkward to hold, particularly when sawing the last few rings from a coil. A recent modification has improved the design in terms of ergonomics and ease of use.

The same groove has been carved at a diagonal angle into a spare bench pin to make sawing much more comfortable.

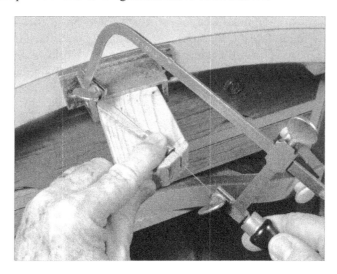

As with the straight block, just thread the saw blade through the coil, place it in the groove against the stop, and saw at an angle.

The groove can be roughed out with a ball bur and finished up with a chisel or pocket knife, but if you know a woodworker, it goes much faster with a power saw.

Having the block held to the bench with an angled groove gives more productivity with less fatigue.

LUBRICATING DRILLS AND BURS

Drilling and burring operations go much quicker with a little lubrication. It helps to reduce the heat caused by friction of the tool against the workpiece, and on a deep hole it helps to clear the chips. Lube oils and cutting oils are familiar products around the workbench. Old-time jewelers used to like Oil of Wintergreen. But an open container of oil often makes a mess if it spills.

One safe way of keeping the oil handy, especially if you travel to classes or workshops, is to put it into a small wide-mouth bottle that has a cotton ball or cosmetic sponge in it. Then even if knocked over, the oil does not spill out.

MAKING A TEXTURE HAMMER

An inexpensive hammer can be easily turned into a great texturing tool by grinding a pattern of narrow lines into its face. The tool I like to use to grind the pattern is a thin separating disc in the Foredom or Dremel. Be sure to hold the hammer and abrasive disc steady as you carve, and wear those safety glasses to protect the eyes.

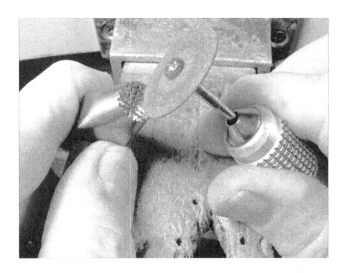

For the pattern to work well, a major part of the face needs to be ground away leaving only small areas of high points. That way the high points will have enough force to emboss the pattern into the sheet metal.

My preference is to use small hammers for this project, either ball peen or cross peen work well. They are quite inexpensive from tool dealers at swap meets and rock and mineral shows. There is no reason to buy an expensive hammer to experiment with creating your own textures. And if you don't like the first try at a pattern, simply file or grind it off and try a second pattern.

RESURFACING A HAMMER

Bringing a hammer face back into good shape is much the same as polishing a silver casting. The surface is filed to shape, then sanded to remove all the file marks, and finally polished to the quality needed for its intended use.

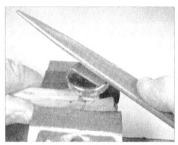 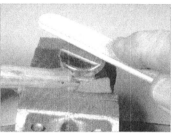

The process is the same for a hammer that has received a few dings in heavy use, a yard sale bargain that needs a little love, or a common ball peen that you want to reshape for a special task.

Once formed to the desired shape, the working surfaces can be kept bright and shiny with an occasional buffing on the Zam or Tripoli wheel.

PREVENTING RUST ON TOOLS

An occasional oiling should be all that's needed to prevent rust from starting to form on tools or on equipment in the shop. Keep a piece of oily cotton cloth to wipe down hand tools, design stamps, shot dies, and such. It's also useful to wipe down a piece of larger equipment. When not in use, just store the cloth in a closed plastic container.

Some shop environments seem to be more prone to rust than others. So if rust is a common occurrence in your shop, there's an old machine shop trick of covering tools and equipment at the end of the work day with a cloth or piece of towel that has some oil on it. I use this technique with expensive equipment like the rolling mill, the anvil, and a surface plate.

SANDING STICKS

One of the tools that saves me so much time when finishing a piece is a common sanding stick used to do your fingernails. I use them like a file. They are inexpensive, sold at local stores, and come in a variety of grits.

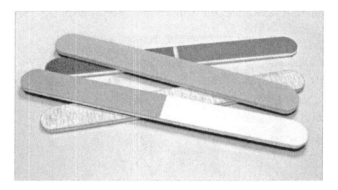

These sanding sticks come as a single grit, a different grit on each side, or four different grits on a stick. The ones with four grits are great for polishing off a minor scratch when you don't have access to all your shop tools. The finest grit must be 1000 or higher.

SINUSOIDAL STAKE FROM CUTTING BOARD

Synclastic or anticlastic forms are often used when making bracelets to give the strength needed while conserving the weight of precious metal. A synclastic shape can be developed with a simple, rounded cavity in a block of wood while the anticlastic shape requires a special stake to support the metal while it is being bent. These sinusoidal stakes are made from steel and can be quite expensive.

However, it's possible to make anticlastic bracelet stake from a piece of thick plastic. For years I used one made from a section of ½ inch thick cutting board, but to show the process here, I'm using a scrap of polycarbonate from a local plastics store. The ½ inch thickness is suitable for 1 inch wide bracelets, but thicker material would be better for wider bracelets.

 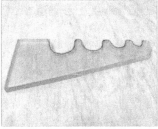

Sketch out a series of circular grooves that span the degree of curve desired. Here I traced several items from ½ inch diameter up to 1 ¾ inch diameter. Cut out the curves with a band saw or coarse saw blade, and then file them to shape and sand smooth with a sanding drum in the flexshaft. Also file the edges of the bottom of the curves to approximate the overall diameter of the bracelet being formed.

Clamp the stake in a sturdy vise, place the bracelet strip into the form, and hammer just off the far edge of the stake to generate the anticlastic shape.

SQUARE

Good layout techniques involve numerous 90 degree angles, and using the larger squares sold for carpenters is cumbersome on the smaller jewelry items we work on. A small two-inch square has become one of my "must have" tools. It's handy to have one in every tool box and a couple at the bench at home.

Chapter 6

CASTING AND MOLDING TIPS

CASTING AN ORGANIC

For something a little different, try casting an organic. I've had good success with twigs, pieces of bark, and small pine cones. The process is straightforward. On the first heat, I melt out any sprue wax and then go to max temperature (1250 F for my investment) to burn out all the organics. Then after an overnight cool-down, I shake or vacuum out the ash and do a regular re-heat to casting temperature before casting as usual.

There are two problems to consider - getting the ash out and dealing with thin sections or stems. When spruing an organic, it's important to make it easy for the ash from the model to fall out through the sprue. If any ash is left in the mold, the metal will not fill all the detail. Sometimes it's necessary to hold the flask over your head and snake a fine wire up the sprue to break up a piece of ash and let it fall out. Be sure to wear safety glasses if you do this.

Thin sections of some organics can be a problem, so things like a broad leaf or a flower petal are risky. Even if they do cast well, (and I have done an orchid) there is little extra metal to allow for clean-up and polishing. It's best to look for elements that are a little thicker before trying leaves and flowers.

One final note - don't forget that wax items can be added to the organic to complete a model. For instance, a stone setting or bail can be fashioned from wax wire, a void in the organic can be patched with wax, or small pits can be filled with Vaseline.

VACUUM CASTING BLOWOUTS

In the vacuum casting method, a vacuum is applied to the bottom of the hot flask while melted metal is poured in from the top. If the investment at the bottom is too thin or has developed a crack, it can give way allowing the melted metal to be drawn down into the machine. Such a blowout of hot metal and investment will clog pipes, fill hoses, and sometimes destroy valves.

Usually the problem is fixed by disassembling the piping, fishing out the debris, and replacing clogged hose sections with new vacuum tubing from an auto parts store. But occasionally, a blowout will shoot molten metal into the control valve - an expensive and time consuming fix.

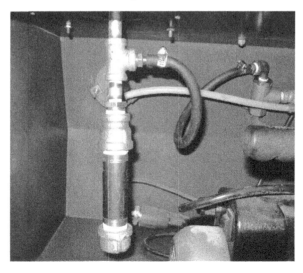

To prevent this happening again, I made up a trap just under the vacuum table to catch all investment and metal. It uses a few pipe fittings and reducing bushings easily available in a good hardware store. Since then, all of my student blowouts have been fixed in about ten minutes and their silver recovered for the next casting.

INGOT MOLDS

Ingot molds are great for converting clean scrap silver into useful bar or sheet material. However, the common steel molds have three limitations that can cause problems. First is that most molds have fairly narrow funnels on the top that can be hard to hit when pouring the metal. Secondly, the steel absorbs heat from the silver so quickly that fills are often incomplete or are in sections that are not completely bonded. And thirdly, there are only a few variations of mold size commercially available.

I had a project to make a number of stamped silver bracelets from 10 gauge bar stock about 20mm wide. This might be available on special order, but I found it quicker and easier to make an ingot mold out of two pieces of 1/2 inch graphite. The mold has a generous sized funnel on the top and so far has not produced any incomplete ingots.

The Internet is a good source for graphite. I used a 6 inch square piece of ½ inch thick material sawed down the middle to make two equally sized pieces 3" x 6" A wood saw or a jewelers saw works nicely. Be sure to use a dust mask and maybe even do it outside. Sawing or carving graphite is quite messy.

The slot in this mold is 110mm long and 15mm wide. Draw out the slot and use a bur, file and scraper to form it to size. Be careful to not cut too deep. Level the bottom of the slot with a file, the edge of a thick sheet of steel, or the cutting edge of a wood chisel.

Make up the mold by clamping or binding the two pieces together. Finally, carve a widened funnel at the top to make it easy to hit the slot when pouring.

Note that like steel, graphite molds must be heated before pouring, but only enough to evaporate any water that may be in the mold. Residual water can create a steam explosion when hot metal hits it.

One way to set up for the pour is to place the mold in a metal pan or used food can and fill in around the mold with one-inch pebbles. That holds the mold securely for use, contains any spilled metal, and preserves extra metal for reuse on the next pour. Be sure to set the pan on a heat resistant surface because any spill will heat the pan enough to scorch a wooden bench.

NEW MELTING DISH

A new melting dish or crucible should be given a protective coating of borax before its first use. Borax extends the life of the ceramic material. Once done, it generally does not have to be repeated unless some holes in the coating develop.

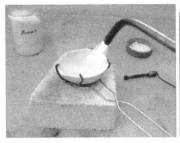

The procedure is straightforward. Heat the new melting dish to red in an oven or with a large torch. You'll need plenty of heat. Shown above is a Prest-O-Lite acetylene/air torch with a large #5 nozzle.

When the dish is hot, sprinkle in a half teaspoon of borax, let it melt, and spread it with a steel or carbon rod over all of the interior surface of the dish. Add more borax if needed.

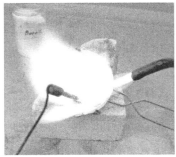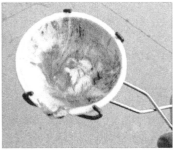

Sometimes you will have to hold the dish at an angle to coat the sides up to the rim. Be sure to coat the pouring spout itself.

HEAT PROOF BENCH SURFACE

An inexpensive and very effective heat proof surface for a soldering or casting area can be made using a building material called Hardie Backer Board. It's a fiber reinforced cement sheet that is typically used as a waterproof base for ceramic tiles in bath tubs and shower stalls. Most lumber yards and home fix-it stores carry the material. Cutting it requires a masonry blade on a circular saw. Be sure to wear a mask and use eye protection when sawing.

STIRRING ROD

When melting metals for casting, it's important to have something to stir the melt. A graphite rod is inexpensive, stands up well to high temperatures, and will not contaminate the metal. Stirring the melt ensures a homogeneous mixture and also lets you check for any lumps of metal that have not yet melted.

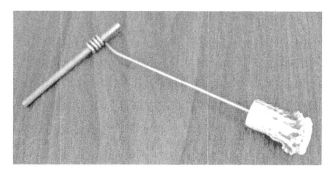

The main problem with a graphite rod is how to hold it. A pair of pliers will work, but graphite is fragile. It is easy to crack a rod, and it usually breaks if dropped.

A simple rod holder can be made from a piece of heavy wire. 3/16 or 1/8 inch steel wire or brass brazing rod works well. Other alternatives are available in most local hardware stores.

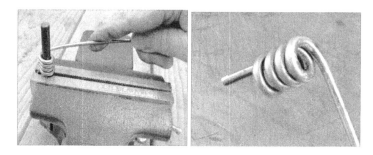

Wind the wire around a mandrel of the right size like you would wind jump rings. Here I used a 15/64 inch mandrel to develop a coil to hold a 1/4 inch graphite rod. Bend the end of the rod down between the vice jaws to keep the coil from turning on the mandrel as you wind the coil.

Chapter 7

EQUIPMENT TIPS

AVOIDING BUFFER MESS

Buffing is one of the dirtier operations in making jewelry, and if you work inside the home, buffer mess from lint and polish can be a big problem. One solution is to buy a dust collecting system, but they can be large, noisy, and expensive.

A more economical approach is to use the 3-M Radial Bristle Disc system rather than cloth wheels. They come as 6 ply wheels in 2 inch or 3 inch diameters. The blue (400 grit) does a nice job at pre-polishing, the peach (6 micron) begins the polishing, and the light green (1 micron) works well for final polishing.

Dust and lint from buffing are minimal, and a side benefit is that there's no waxy grime to wash off between grit levels.

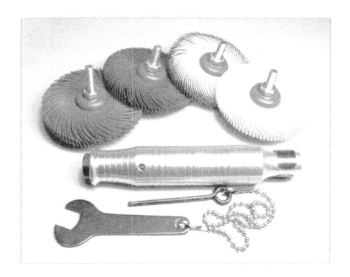

Radial Bristle wheels can be mounted on a regular buffer equipped with a tapered spindle or can be mounted on larger 1/4 inch mandrels and used in the Foredom #25 or H.44T handpieces. The wheels shown above use ¼ inch bolts and nuts as mandrels.

It's always best to wear goggles and a mask while buffing to avoid the fine metal particles that are being thrown into the air.

INEXPENSIVE PICKLE BASKET

The pickle pot used in our classroom is an old, slow-cooking pot from a yard sale such as used by many jewelers. Retrieving small parts from the bottom is difficult without some form of basket.

Replacement baskets for commercial pots are quite pricey, so I was very pleased to find a local source of stainless steel baskets with a handle for about $6. It's a nice size, about 3 inches in diameter.

Some stainless steels will react with the pickle to coat things with copper, and others will not. This basket is made from a good quality stainless steel that shows no reaction at all.

In case you're interested, one supplier is:

- Jewelry Tools & Supplies
- 412 W. 6th Street #1011
- Los Angeles, CA 90014
- 213 624-8224
- jtstech@sbcglobal.net

NO SCRATCH VISE JAWS

If a bench vise has replaceable jaws, there is a simple modification to customize it for bending sheet metal and holding jewelry pieces without worrying about the jaws leaving scratch marks.

Make a duplicate set of jaws from high density plastic such as Nylon or Delrin. Remove the steel jaws and use them as a template. Cut two pieces from a 1/2 inch sheet of scrap plastic. Then clamp the steel jaw over the plastic and drill through the steel side and into the plastic. Finally, use a larger drill to countersink the plastic for the screw heads.

Plastic can be obtained from the scrap bin at a local plastics store, can be purchased online from Ebay, or can be repurposed from an old kitchen cutting board.

ONE PART DIE FORMING

An easy way to make large and strong components for your jewelry designs while keeping the weight of precious metal to a minimum is done with simple tools in a process called one-part die forming. Complex 3-D shapes can be made quickly from thin gauge sheet with just a piece of plastic and a dapping ball.

A forming die can be made by sketching the shape needed on a piece of thick plastic. Then drill a hole and saw out the shape with a jeweler's saw and a coarse blade. When sawing, try to keep edges straight up and down. Refine the cut as needed with a sanding drum or file. Select a thickness of plastic that is just a little more than the amount of doming you want.

Note: I tend to use 1/4 inch or 3/8 inch plastic which can be found as scraps from a local plastics shop or in a search on the Internet.

To use the die, cut a piece of sheet metal about 1/2 inch wider than the hole in the die on all sides. Anneal the sheet and tape it down on the plastic. Use a dapping ball and hammer to create the domed shape. When the taped down edges begin to warp, planish them flat on the top of the die. Finally, if the sheet is to be domed deeply, you will need to anneal the metal occasionally.

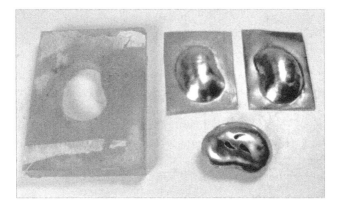

A nice feature of this technique can be seen in the top left of the picture. If the sawed walls of the die are straight up and down, the hole on the bottom is a mirror image of the hole on the top. This allows you to produce mirror image shapes as needed to make left and right earrings or both sides of an irregular shaped bead as shown on the bottom right.

SELECTING A BENCH VISE

In selecting a bench vise, what features are the most important for the kind of work jewelers do? A bench vise is one of the tools that should last for a lifetime. Now is not the time to look for a bargain basement cost saver.

A main criteria is that it should be sturdy and be of the size needed for the work typically done. I prefer a vise that is bolted to the bench and has at least4 inch wide jaws.

Secondly, if the vise will be used to hold round tools, like a ring mandrel, it's worth looking for one that has pipe jaws built into the throat of the vise. They are designed to hold cylindrical shapes securely when hammering.

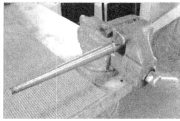

A third consideration is the jaws themselves. It is important to have replaceable jaws because jewelers use a vise in many different ways. For holding a forming tool, steel jaws with heavy serrations are needed to hold a tool rigidly. For fold forming, flat jaws work best for bending and forging without leaving marks on the sheet metal. So look for a vise that has replaceable jaws with serrations on one side and a flat surface on the other side.

A final consideration before purchasing is the overall quality of manufacture. The clamping screw and the horizontal swivel mechanism of the vise should work smoothly.

MAKE A BUFFER

An inexpensive buffer can be made from a used motor or a yard sale bench grinder. Look for a motor that is at least 1/4 horsepower with a shaft that is 1/2 or 5/8 inch diameter. Motors with a speed of 1750 rpm and ideally with a shaft at both ends are useful.

To make the buffer, purchase a tapered screw adaptor to fit the shaft. See Rio Grande part numbers 333042 through 333051 at about $7 each. Choose the side you like to work on - right or left.

DRILL KEY

Keep your chuck key from getting lost with a length of chain or small gauge plastic coated wire rope. The cable shown here is one millimeter stranded steel wire rope that is coated with nylon or vinyl plastic. The coating has an outer diameter of about 1/16 inch.

Connections are easily made to the drill key and the equipment with 1/16 inch cable splicing sleeves/crimps. You can purchase a small amount of the wire rope and matching cable crimps on the Internet and it has solved a number of problems around the shop.

RUST REMOVAL

When tools start to show some rust, usually a fine steel wire brush followed by a coat of lubricating oil does the trick. If any areas need more work, try steel wool and oil.

A tool that has rusted quite a bit can still be saved. The first step is to remove all the coarse flaky rust with a wire brush, either by hand or with a brush mounted on a buffer or electric drill.

Wire brushes are readily available online or from local hardware stores. This is a messy job, so do it outside if possible and wear good safety goggles. Finish up with a little sanding or scraping where needed.

A new product called EvapoRust has given very good results for removing the last traces of rust. It's available at local auto parts stores. The product works well, is reusable, has no acids in it, and produces no fumes.

- Cover the parts with EvapoRust for an hour
- Wipe clean and inspect
- Work on remaining spots with fine sandpaper or steel wool
- Submerge again in EvapoRust if necessary
- Dry the parts and wipe down with an oily rag

BAND SAW

I originally purchased a small band saw to cut exotic woods for some jewelry items and have found so many uses for it in the shop.

If you are so inclined, there are three things to look for in this type of equipment.

You will need to use a fine toothed blade of 24-30 teeth per inch or more for cutting sheet metal smoothly without a lot of vibration. Check for availability of these blades before buying the saw.

If you wish to be able to cut curves with the saw, You will need a blade that is narrow, perhaps 1/8 inch. Check for availability of these blades also before buying the saw.

Thirdly, only a small saw will be needed, and the critical specification is called throat distance - the widest metal strip you can cut without the end bumping into the saw structure. Think of a jewelers hand saw. Sometimes a 2 or 3 inch saw frame works well. Other times a larger 4 or 5 inch frame is needed so that the metal doesn't hit the back side of the saw frame. I feel a band saw for the jewelry shop should have at least a 6 inch throat distance.

TESTING AN ANVIL

Anvils that are made from inexpensive material like cast iron are softer than a hammer and are liable to get dinged up during normal use. A good anvil has a hardened surface, harder than a hammer, to keep it smooth over years of use. The body of good anvils will also be made from better quality steel and not from cheaper cast iron.

There are no easy ways to check for the hardness of steel without some expensive equipment. But there are some quick tests that will give an indication. An anvil with a hardened surface and a quality steel body will give a high pitched ring when hit with a hammer. A cheaper or cracked anvil will give a heavy "thunk" when hit. Another indicator of hardness is to drop a large steel ball bearing on the anvil. The higher it bounces back, the better the quality of the anvil.

WAX PEN TIPS

A good tool for wax fabrication is an electric pen that stays at constant temperature. The controller is a simple commercial device used for dimming a light or controlling the speed of a tool, and the "pen" itself is an inexpensive 25 watt soldering iron available at Harbor Freight and other suppliers.

Tips on the soldering iron are replaceable, so they can be custom shaped to suit the work - different shaped tips for different tasks. Here are a couple that are useful.

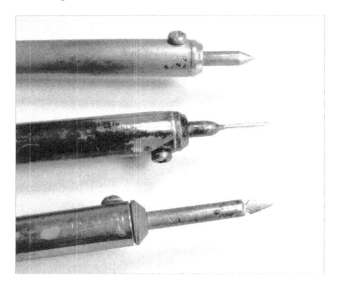

The long (15mm - 16ga) needle like tip in the center lets me reach deep into a model or wax tree. However, because it's so long, a steel or brass wire is not able to conduct enough heat to the tip. Silver is a great heat conductor and works well in this application.

SHARPENING A BLADE

A simple oilstone will keep cutting edges sharp with a minimum of effort. One side is generally a medium abrasive for restoring the shape of a blade that has been nicked or damaged, and the other side is a very fine abrasive to sharpen the actual cutting edge.

When using an oilstone, clean any debris from the surface, spread a little lubricating oil on it, hold the blade at a shallow 15 degree angle, and stroke the blade towards you as if to cut into the oilstone. Then repeat with the other side of the blade. Sharpening a pen knife is done in much the same way.

WIRE GAUGE

Jewelers use the Brown & Sharpe Non-Ferrous gauging system for measuring precious metals in the U.S.A. Gauges are stamped either "B&S Non-Ferrous" or "American Standard" to indicate compliance. They are typically a three inch diameter steel disk with numbered slots around the outside.

These thickness gauges are not cheap, and if you try to buy a used one from a tool sale or from eBay, be careful that the gauge is marked B&S Non-Ferrous or American Standard. There are two other thickness measuring systems in use with similarly shaped round gauges that will not measure precious metals correctly. They measure in the Brown & Sharp Ferrous gauging system and in the British Standard gauging system.

Chapter 8

SAFETY TIPS

DRILLING JIG

One common hazard when drilling a hole in a small piece of sheet metal is the drill catching in the cut. If the sheet is not held firmly when that happens, the metal can spin around and cut your finger.

Good shop practice of course is to clamp the workpiece while drilling or use a small vise or some pliers to hold it securely, but too frequently the warnings are ignored.

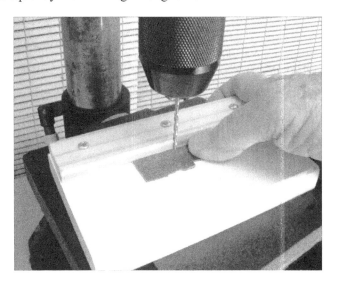

A simple drilling jig can be made from a length of board and a strip of molding to prevent the sheet metal from spinning. Leave this jig on the drill press so it's always handy. The board provides a level seat for through-hole drilling, and the molding prevents the workpiece from spinning clockwise with the drill.

SHOP VENTILATION

Any equipment that sucks air and discharges it back into your work-space should have both a filter for dust particles and a filter for soldering vapors in order to be effective. It will be easy to see when the dust filter needs replacement, but the vapor filter will not have a visual clue as to when it has lost its effectiveness.

Vapor filters typically make use of activated charcoal. They don't last too long, and they're not inexpensive to replace. Be sure to follow the unit's instructions. If not done correctly, the vapors from soldering will not be trapped. They just pass right through, and you will be fooling yourself into thinking that the unit is protecting your lungs.

The best solution is to exhaust fumes from the soldering area to the outside of the building. Some folks use an old kitchen range hood as an effective, low-cost option. You don't necessarily have to cut a hole in the wall if you can exhaust the 4 or 6 inch duct through a window opening. An easy way is to replace one of the window panes with a piece of plastic that has a hole cut in it for the exhaust duct. A handy-man or mechanically inclined friend might be able to help.

Chapter 9

PROJECT PLANNING TIPS

DIVIDERS

A set of dividers is a tool I find very useful in laying out the geometry of a piece I'm making. It has two needle-like tips with an adjustment to set the spacing between them.

They can be used to transfer a measurement. Let's say you need a 7mm wide strip of sheet metal. Set the spacing between the divider tips to 7 mm on the ruler. Then lay the sheet on the bench, put one tip against the edge, and run the dividers down the edge scribing a line parallel to the edge.

Dividers can be used to mark equal segments of a line or arc. For instance, assume a line between A and B that might be straight or curved, and you want to divide it into 5 equal lengths. Set the dividers to an estimate of the distance. Starting at Point A, use the dividers to mark off five lengths along the line. If you end up short of Point B, lengthen the distance on the dividers. If you end up overshooting Point B, shorten the length of your dividers. After a few tries, the length on the dividers will be the exact distance you need to mark the 5 segments.

Dividers can let you quickly find the center of a circular disk. With one tip of the dividers at the edge of the disk, set the other tip to an estimate of where the center might be. Fix one tip of the dividers at the 3 o'clock position and scribe an arc with the other tip near the center. Do this again from the 6 o'clock, 9 o'clock, and 12 o'clock positions. The arcs at the center will form a small four-sided box. The center of the box is at the center of the disk.

DESIGN STAMP LAYOUT

One of the problems in using metal stamps is laying out the design to get the right alignment and spacing. One way to experiment with different layouts is to press the stamp onto an inked stamp pad and transfer its shape onto a sketch of your design.

A second way is to use the aluminum foil tape that is sold in local building supplies stores for sealing air conditioning ducts.

But the best way I have found to try different layouts is to use modeling clay rolled out flat.

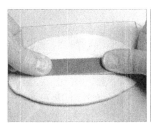 

If you are using a pre-cut metal shape, a stone, or a bezel, press that into the clay to leave an outline as a guide. Then experiment with spacing the design stamps around it. The design stamps show clearly when pressed into the clay.

REDESIGN FOR PRODUCIBILITY

Minor re-designs in a product can make the piece more easy or more inexpensive to produce. Look for components or subassemblies than can be done by casting. And look for sheet metal component shapes that can be cut with a pancake die (sometimes this entails minor changes to the outer shape).

Special Tooling - Next, make up things like templates, gauges, jigs, and even forming dies that will reduce the time needed to shape, position, or size components of the piece.

Reduce Setup Time - It takes time to assemble all the tools and equipment to do a job. This is called set-up time, and you want to minimize it. Take good notes while you work of the tools you used and the sequence of operations. Also note where you buy some of the odd materials, the lengths you cut, etc. This makes it easier to get everything together for the next time you have to make up the same piece.

Batch Production - Lastly, try to do your work in batches. Make 4, 8, or a dozen at a time rather than just one. Complete each operation on all pieces in the batch before moving on to the next operation. That way, there is only one set-up time for all pieces in the batch. For instance, you spend 8 minutes clearing the bench & bench pin, finding the 3" saw frame, selecting the right saw blades, and searching for some lube wax. Then you saw all the pieces from the sheet.

Chapter 10

MISCELLANEOUS TIPS

QUICK CLOSE-UPS

Often when trying to get a close-up photo with a smart phone, the lens will not focus as closely enough. If a jewelers loupe is available, try holding it over the camera lens. It works quickly and easily.

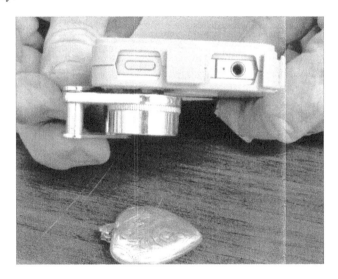

CLEANING SILVER

The tarnish on silver items exposed to sulfur-based air pollutants can be cleaned using a Pyrex dish lined with aluminum foil. Place the silver on the foil. In a large sauce pan, heat 1 cup water, 1 tbsp salt, and1 tbsp baking soda. Bring near a boil, pour into the dish, and let stand for 15-20 minutes.

>> Not recommended for jewelry with fragile stones like opal, pearls, amber, turquoise, and others.

FINDING A JEWELRY CLASS

Check the art department class schedule at local community colleges.

Also check to see if there is a gem and mineral club nearby. Club members often make jewelry and should know about any local classes. Some clubs have their own shop and teach informal classes. For instance, the Culver City Rock and Mineral Club has a fully equipped shop open to members five times a week. And the often have organized workshop sessions for their members.

To find a rock and gem club in your area, do an Internet search for "gem mineral club" along with your Zip Code or see some of the contact addresses in the Appendix.

GLUED DOP STICKS

Dop sticks are wood or metal rods used as a "handle" to hold small stones while they are being shaped and polished. The rough gem material is usually fastened onto the dop stick with a wax. The stick is dipped into hot dopping wax, the stone is heated to the same temperature, and the stone is positioned on the end of the rod while the wax hardens.

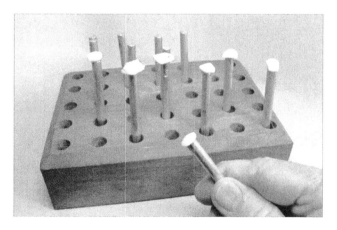

But some stones, such as many opals, are very sensitive to heat. To avoid problems I often use super glue to mount my fragile stones onto short lengths of aluminum rod. It's quick and secure.

To release the stones, I place the dop, stone-side down ,into a screw-top bottle, pour in enough acetone to cover the glue joint, and screw on the cap. The glue starts to give way in several hours.

HOLIDAY SALES

Some of the best times to sell your jewelry are just before major holidays such as Christmas, Valentines Day and Mothers Day. But with booth rent at some shows getting pretty pricey, a home-based jeweler has to get creative to find a place to sell their pieces. Often a friend can host a gift party for you. And it pays to be on the alert for local shows at community centers, street fairs, and church bazaars.

If there are no shows available as a holiday approaches, ask a few friends who work in the administrative area of large companies if they might be interested in hosting a holiday jewelry party in one of their conference rooms at lunchtime. This lets you bring in your pieces and show them off to a captive audience. And it costs you nothing - no booth fees or table rentals.

If you don't have enough pieces to fill a couple tables, ask if you can invite one or two of your jewelry friends to participate with you. (make sure their line does not compete with yours).

Put together a short email flyer about the event with a picture or two that your friend can use to craft an announcement to send out to the office distribution list (ask to be copied on it).

And if you find you like shows, be sure to call around to everyone in your area to develop a list of show possibilities for next year. You'll need to know who's in charge, the dates, costs, and special requirements for things like contracts, business licenses, sales tax numbers, fire code, liability insurance, etc.

HALLMARKS

When trying to identify an object that might be precious metal, jewelers always look first for a hallmark stamp. Any item made from silver or gold should be marked as such, and each country has its own rules as to how that should be done. Some marks are familiar, like "14K", "925" or "Sterling", but other marks are used to identify different alloys, like Argentium or Platinum, or metals that are not homogeneous, like gold filled or Sterling filled wire and sheet.These purity marks are called Hallmarks.

Many beginning students think it is unnecessary to mark their pieces with the metal used because they will remember it. But if the piece is then sold or given away, the information about the metals used is quickly lost. That's why it's best practice to mark all pieces. Hallmark stamps are available from all your favorite jewelry supply companies.

Some silver pieces will have other types of marks as well. These identify where or when the object was created. A good reference for identifying these marks is the Online Encyclopedia of Silver Marks, Hallmarks, and Maker's Marks at http://www.925-1000.com/index.html

QUALITY GEMSTONES

Online shopping for tools & supplies is quick and easy, but buying a nice cabochon online is difficult for me. I like to be able to see the stone, handle it, and be inspired by its shape, size, color, weight, pattern, and luster.

Few of us have local sources for gemstones, and many cannot travel to the large venues like the Tucson shows. So where can you find a good selection of gemstones? For many of us, local rock and mineral club shows offer a good selection of vendors with a wide range of material. You'll find slabs, cabs, faceted stones, beads, tools, finished jewelry, supplies, and displays of collections and handmade items by club members.

To find a rock & gem club in your area, do an Internet search for "gem mineral club" along with your Zip Code or see some of the contact addresses in the Appendix.

MAKER'S MARK

One of the basic lessons in jewelry is the importance of stamping your work, not only for the metal content but also to identify the artist with a Maker's mark. Marks vary from simple text fonts to more elaborate artistic logos.

Here are several sources that can create a custom Maker's stamp for you with your name, initials or logo. To get a quote, just send a .pdf of the text you want or artwork of your logo. Your clients and family will appreciate knowing positively that a piece was created by you.

Buckeye Engraving in Kent, OH
http://buckeyeengraving.com
stamps@buckeyeengraving.com

Ever Stamps in Providence, RI
http://www.henryaevers.com
everstamp@aol.com

Ferro Valley Tool in Albuquerque, NM
http://www.ferrovalleytools.com
ferrovalleytool@gmail.com

Microstamp in Pasadena, CA
http://www.microstamp.us
quotes@microstamp.us

Steel Stamps in Boise, ID
http://www.harpermfg.com
info@harpermfg.com

There are two things that are important to specify when ordering a makers mark stamp – the height of the stamp and the shape of the stamp shank. A reasonable starting point for the height of text on the stamp is about 1.6mm for capital letters and about 1.0mm for small letters. Stamp shanks can be ordered in round or square shapes. I think the square shank makes it a lot easier to align the stamp on the piece of jewelry before striking the mark.

RTV MOLD FRAME

Inexpensive mold frames are available from jewelry supply companies for making a mold with 2-part RTV compounds. But if the right size is not available, a custom mold frame can be made with a piece of 1/8 inch thick aluminum bar stock from a local hardware store or metals supplier.

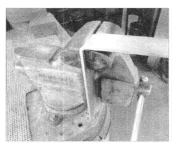 

Bend the aluminum in a bench vise to form a flat bottom "U" shape with the width and height you need.

Mold frames need to be 0.5 to .75 inch wider on both sides of the model being molded to avoid leakage when using the finished mold. The frame also needs to be at least 2 inches taller than the level of RTV compound being poured into it. This allows for expansion of the compound during vacuum debubbling.

Finish up the mold frame by filing or sanding both sides flat to ensure a good fit with the plastic sheets that will form the sides. The plastic should overlap the frame by a quarter inch on all sides. Lastly, attach a sprue former to the center of the bottom.

A sprue former is a conical shape about 1/2 inch in diameter with two functions. First, it provides a 1/8 inch hole for attaching the sprued model to the mold frame. Secondly, the conical shape forms a funnel in the finished rubber mold that is designed to fit the nozzle of a wax injector.

Sprue formers can be purchased from jewelry tools suppliers for about $5, or can be made from a piece of plastic. Mount the sprue former to the aluminum frame with a #8 flush head threaded screw or a bit of super glue or epoxy.

APPENDIX

INTERNET RESOURCES

http://www.Foredom.netThe Foredom® Company

http://www.Dremel.comThe Dremel® Company

http://EGGMenterprises.comEGGM Enterprises, Torrance, CA

http://www.FDJtool.com   FDJ On Time, Winter Park, FL

http://www.LascoDiamond.comLasco Diamond, Calabassas, CA

http://www.OttoFrei.comOtto Frei Jewelry, San Francisco, CA

http://www.RioGrande.comRio Grande, Albuquerque, NM

FINDING A ROCK & MINERAL CLUB

Some countries have federations to organize their rock and mineral clubs. Here is a list of the ones I know:

Australia:
- http://www.mineral.org.au/clubs/clubs.html

- http://aflaca.org.au/members/gem-and-mineral-clubs-association-of-south-australia-gmcasa/

Canada:
- http://www.ccfms.ca/Online_Resources/online_clubs.htm

Namibia:
- http://fosagams.co.za/walvisbay/

New Zealand:
- http://www.cmlclub.evanta.co.nz/new-zealand-rock-and-mineral-clubs/

South Africa:
- http://www.fosagams.co.za/galleries/photo-gallery/south-african-gem-mineral-club-pe

UK:
-
http://www.srbstones.co.uk/Clubs%20and%20Societies/clubs%20and%20societies.htm

-
 http://csmsgeologypost.blogspot.com/2014/03/united-kingdom-rock-mineral-clubs.html

-
http://www.geologistsassociation.org.uk/affiliatedandlocalgroups.html

USA:
- http://amfed.org/club.htm

ABOUT THE AUTHOR

Brad Smith is a studio jeweler, lapidary, and jewelry instructor in Santa Monica, CA. He enjoys working with silver, gold, exotic woods, bone, fossil ivory, and meteorite.

As a long-time member of the Culver City Rock Club, Brad has taught lapidary skills, led field trips to the desert, organized gem and mineral shows, and served in most of the club positions, including President. He is also a member of the Metal Arts Society of Southern California.

His teaching career started in the Los Angeles school system where he taught Advanced Jewelry in the Adult Education Department for eight years. Then in 2009, he was invited to design and build a new jewelry facility at the Santa Monica Adult Education Center where he currently teaches beginning and advanced classes.

Brad also likes photography& scuba diving, develops websites, and moderates several jewelry making and rockhounding discussion groups on the Internet.

Contact the author at
BradSmithJewelry @gmail.com

or see his website at

http://BradSmithJewelry.com/

OTHER BOOKS BY THE AUTHOR

Making Design Stamps for Jewelry

Learn how to create unique stamps and texturing tools to add visual interest to your work, for a special application, or to brand your pieces with a stamp that others cannot purchase. These customized tools embellish your jewelry designs and can be made with common jewelry tools and techniques. There are only a few differences in working with steel as compared to copper or silver.

The volume covers the step-by-step process of selecting best steels, carving the design, hardening the steel, and tempering it to ensure a long service life. It describes the tools to use, gives detailed examples for making several stamps, includes sources for tool steel, describes useful shop equipment, and has tips for saving time and achieving better quality.

amazon.com/dp/098828586X/

Editorial Review

"A must have book for the metalsmith"
- Danny Wade, Ferro Valley Tool, LLC and
creator of the Metal Stamp Addicts group on Facebook.

Amazon Reader Review

- This book is absolutely wonderful! If you are at all interested in the very least in making your own jewelry stamps, then you definitely need this book. At 68 pages, I was initially hesitant, but I was wrong; this book is jam-packed with a plethora of information, all of which is totally relevant, and revealing.

Accessories for the Foredom and Dremel

Flexible shaft and motor tools are an indispensable help to those who make jewelry, improving both the productivity and the quality of work. But with such an array of different tool bits to choose from, it's sometimes difficult to figure out the best one to use for each task.

"Accessories for the Foredom and Dremel" surveys the range of tool bits available for use with flexible shaft and hand-held motor tools and discusses the merits of each.

It highlights the best drill bits to use, the three most useful cutting burs, six different types of sanding bits, five ways to polish your work with the Foredom or Dremel, and five bits that can be used to add texture. In each category, I share my experience with the tool bits which save the most time, mention bench tips for getting the best results, and add cautions for safe use.

amazon.com/dp/0988285878/

Amazon Reader Reviews

- Five Stars - What a little treasure! … This book, while small, is packed full of great information on the subject. It's a great resource to keep handy at your bench.

- Five Stars - This is a wonderful book from someone that knows what he's talking about. Excellent tips and knowledge along the way.

- Five Stars - Love this book! Great reference book. Mr. Smith does a very good job of explaining how to choose the best tool bits for each job and how to use them to the best advantage. The information is very clearly written and well organized. I would definitely recommend this book to anyone interested in metalworking.

Broom Casting For Creative Jewelry

Discover the rush of pouring molten silver into a straw broom to get marvelous icicle-like shapes that just beg to be designed into finished jewelry like pendants and earrings.

Broom casting is a technique that yields beautiful results, doesn't require a lot of time to learn, and is just plain fun to do. In a couple hours you can be producing intriguing geometries that spark the imagination and challenge your creativity.

"Broom Casting For Creative Jewelry" gives step-by-step procedures for casting and covers proper use of all equipment. It includes how to work with the irregular shapes for your designs and has suggestions for safety, tips for cleaning & polishing, and ideas for making some of your own tools. Other sections cover how to run your own broom casting workshop for friends & club members and a gallery of finished jewelry utilizing some of the cast shapes.

amazon.com/dp/0988285835/

Amazon Reader Reviews

- I've found Broom Casting a little intimidated, but I love the look. So I was really excited to hear about this book. Brad Smith's book really takes the mystery out of the process. He breaks down the steps really well, and walks you through the process clearly and simply. Then he shows you how to look at, clean/cut, and finally create with the castings. He really covers this cool technique from top to bottom. It's all in this great little book.

- Broom Casting for Creative Jewelry and Metal Work outlines everything you need to know to start and continue broom casting silver.

Bench Tips for Jewelry Making – Book 1

In every field, the top artisans have their favorite ways of solving common problems. Making a piece of fine jewelry is no exception. Accomplished jewelers have a variety of techniques, special tools and shortcuts that are proven to save time and improve quality.

This book is written as a resource for jewelers with skill levels from beginner through advanced. The bench tips come from Brad Smith's twenty years of experience in the jewelry industry, including over a decade teaching hundreds of students.

The tips include over twenty ways to save time when soldering and polishing, eight common hazards to avoid, many ways to cut costs, ten tips to improve stone setting skills, and the "must-have" tools for increasing productivity at the bench.

amazon.com/dp/0988285800/

Editorial Reviews

This small treasure covers a multitude of solutions to a myriad of issues facing the jewelry artisan...The easy to understand text and very good photographic black and white images makes this book quite self-explanatory...
> - Razine Wenneker - Founder, The Society for Midwest Metalsmiths

This is a well written reference book by a very experienced studio jeweler and classroom instructor. The photographs and diagrams clearly point out the finer points of the various tips he demonstrates...
> - Bruce Carlson - Florida Society of Goldsmiths Newsletter

The Reluctant Farmer of Whimsey Hill- A Memoir

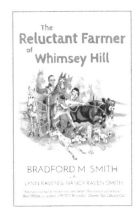

The Reluctant Farmer of Whimsey Hill is a light-hearted, true love story between more than a man and a woman. Imagine *Marley and Me*, not with one pesky dog, but with a farm full of quirky animals. The narrative follows Brad's fish-out-of-water point of view as a 25-year-old, animal-phobic, computer nerd from the city who moves to a rural, Virginia farm with his new, animal-loving bride. There he's propelled on a journey of self-discovery as his bride's crazy animals teach him about life and love - the hard way.

amazon.com/dp/0988285851/

Editorial Reviews

- Animals can and do make our lives better. This is my kind of book.
    - Bret Witter, #1 NYT bestseller and co-author of Dewey [the Library Cat]

- A witty memoir reminding us that the best lessons in life are beyond the edge of one's comfort zone, and one can only be towed there by the heart strings."
    - Jean Abernethy, creator of Fergus the Horse

Amazon Reader Reviews

- Anyone who loves animals, has a sense of humor and appreciates a good, clean book (plenty of mud though) will love this book!

- A charming, witty, well written account of the country life of a young couple, with some sweet moments and some laugh out loud moments. We thoroughly enjoyed it.

Made in the USA
Coppell, TX
20 January 2022

71962964R00056